Hallelujah, What a Savior!

25 Hymn Stories
Celebrating Christ Our Redeemer

KENNETH W. OSBECK

kregel
PUBLICATIONS

Grand Rapids, MI 49501

Hallelujah, What a Savior!:
25 Hymn Stories Celebrating Christ Our Redeemer

© 2000 by Kenneth W. Osbeck

Published by Kregel Publications, a division of Kregel, Inc., P.O. Box 2607, Grand Rapids, MI 49501. Kregel Publications provides trusted, biblical publications for Christian growth and service. Your comments and suggestions are valued.

For more information about Kregel Publications, visit our web site: www.kregel.com

Coverphoto: © by PhotoDisc, Inc. / © by Cleo Photography

ISBN 0-8254-3432-7

Printed in the United States of America

1 2 3 4 5 / 04 03 02 01 00

Contents

Introduction

The most important events in human history—the birth of Christ, His atoning work, and His resurrection—demand our finest songs of praise and celebration. It is fitting, therefore, that some of the noblest music composed has centered on these events. Expressing our beliefs with song makes Christ's redemption more personal and His presence intimately real to us.

In many Christian traditions, Easter is preceded by a forty-day period of spiritual reflection and preparation known as Lent. Holy Week—the seven days preceding Easter Sunday—has been called the week that forever changed the course of history. Without the events of Holy Week, there would be no reconciliation with God and no hope of eternal life. How thrilling to journey with the Lord to Jerusalem on Palm Sunday, to the Upper Room for the Last Supper, to Gethsemane, to Golgotha, and finally to the empty tomb to hear anew the angelic announcement: "He is not here; he has risen just as he said" (Matt. 28:6).

The celebration of Christ's atoning sacrifice must not be limited to just one season of the year nor thoughtlessly changed from a holy day into a holiday. The redemption accomplished through our Savior's death and resurrection ought to be an ongoing, daily experience for every believer. As we walk in obedience to His Word by the indwelling power of the Holy Spirit, we realize more fully the spiritual freedom and blessings that flow from redemption.

The following hymns and their stories may be used in your times of daily devotion. Consider thoughtfully the circumstances that prompted the writing of these proven favorites and let your relationship with Christ be reflected in a "singing faith." A special devotional guide for the Easter season ("From Palm Sunday to Easter") is included, beginning on p. 111.

May the spiritual journey through this week lead you to affirm with the apostle Paul his four basic goals in life as stated in Philippians 3:10:

- to know Christ
- to realize the power of His resurrection
- to share in His sufferings
- to become like Him in His death

Come, Christians, join to sing; Alleluia! Amen!
Loud praise to Christ our King; Alleluia! Amen!
Let all, with heart and voice, before His throne rejoice;
Praise is His gracious choice; Alleluia! Amen!

Praise yet our Christ again; Alleluia! Amen!
Life shall not end the strain; Alleluia! Amen!
On heaven's blissful shore His goodness we'll adore,
Singing forevermore, "Alleluia! Amen!"
            —Christian Henry Bateman

1

Abide with Me

But they constrained him, saying, Abide with us:
for it is toward evening, and the day is far spent.
And he went in to tarry with them.

—Luke 24:29 (KJV)

Abide with Me

HENRY F. LYTE, 1793–1847   WILLIAM H. MONK, 1823–1889

"Eventide"

1. A - bide with me; fast falls the e - ven - tide. The dark-ness
2. Swift to its close ebbs out life's lit - tle day. Earth's joys grow
3. I need Thy pres-ence ev - 'ry pass-ing hour. What but Thy
4. I fear no foe, with Thee at hand to bless; Ills have no
5. Hold Thou Thy cross be - fore my clos-ing eyes; Shine thro' the

deep - ens; Lord, with me a - bide. When oth - er help - ers
dim; its glo - ries pass a - way. Change and de - cay in
grace can foil the tempt-er's pow'r? Who, like Thy - self, my
weight, and tears no bit - ter - ness. Where is death's sting? Where,
gloom, and point me to the skies. Heav'n's morn-ing breaks, and

fail and com-forts flee, Help of the help-less, O a - bide with me.
all a - round I see; O Thou who chang-est not, a - bide with me.
Guide and Stay can be? Thro' cloud and sun-shine, O a - bide with me.
grave, thy vic - to - ry? I tri - umph still if Thou a - bide with me.
earth's vain shad-ows flee. In life, in death, O Lord, a - bide with me.

Yes, life is like the Emmaus road,
  and we tread it not alone
For beside us walks the Son of God,
  to uphold and keep His own.
And our hearts within us thrill with joy
  at His words of love and grace,
And the glorious hope that when the day is done
  we shall see His blessed face.

—Avis B. Christiansen

The inspiration for this lovely hymn's text came while the author, Rev. Henry F. Lyte, was reading Luke 24. Verses 13–35 tell of our Lord's appearance with the two disciples on their seven-mile walk from Jerusalem to the village of Emmaus on Easter Sunday evening:

> And it came to pass, as he sat at meat with them, he took bread, and blessed it, and brake, and gave to them. And their eyes were opened, and they knew him; and he vanished out of their sight. And they said one to another, Did not our heart burn within us, while he talked with us by the way, and while he opened to us the scriptures?
> —Luke 24:30–32 (KJV)

The Emmaus account is always thrilling to read and ponder. How the hearts of those discouraged disciples suddenly burned within them when they realized that they were speaking with the risen, eternal Son of God Himself. After meditating on this account, Henry Lyte prayed: "As Thou dwelt with Thy disciples, Lord, abide with me."

Pastor Lyte ministered faithfully for twenty-three years to a community of poor fishermen at Lower Brixham, in Devonshire, England. During his later years, his health grew progressively worse so that he was eventually forced to seek a warmer climate in Italy. For the last sermon with his parishioners, on September 4, 1847, Lyte almost crawled to the pulpit and delivered his message as though a dying man. His final words made a deep impact upon his people: "It is my desire to induce you to prepare for the solemn hour which must come to all, by a timely appreciation and dependence on the changeless Christ and His death."

"Abide with Me" is thought to have been written shortly before this last service. Before he ever reached Italy, Henry Lyte died at Nice, France, and was buried there in the English cemetery on November 20, 1847.

The tune for Lyte's text, "Eventide," was composed by one of England's leading church musicians of that time, William H. Monk, music editor of the famed Anglican hymnal, *Hymns Ancient and Modern.* "Abide with Me" was included in the first edition of this collection in 1861.

Relive the thrill expressed by the two Emmaus disciples
when their spiritual eyes were opened and they first
realized that they were in the presence of their risen Lord.

2

All Glory, Laud, and Honor

The next day the great crowd that had come for the
Feast heard that Jesus was on his way to Jerusalem.
They took palm branches and went out to meet him,
shouting, "Hosanna!" "Blessed is he who comes in the
name of the Lord!"

—John 12:12–13

All Glory, Laud, and Honor

THEODOLPH OF ORLEANS, 760–821
Trans. JOHN M. NEALE, 1818–1866

MELCHIOR TESCHNER, 1584–1635

"St. Theodolph"

1. All glo-ry, laud, and hon-or To Thee, Re-deem-er, King,
2. The com-pa-ny of an - gels Are prais-ing Thee on high,
3. To Thee, be-fore Thy pas - sion, They sang their hymns of praise—

To whom the lips of chil - dren Made sweet ho-san-nas ring.
And mor-tal men and all things Cre - a - ted make re - ply.
To Thee, now high ex - alt - ed, Our mel - o - dy we raise.

Thou art the King of Is - ra - el, Thou Da - vid's roy - al Son,
The peo - ple of the He - brews With palms be - fore Thee went;
Thou didst ac - cept their prais - es; Ac - cept the praise we bring,

Who in the Lord's name com - est, The King and Bless - ed One.
Our praise and prayer and an - thems Be - fore Thee we pre - sent.
Who in all good de - light - est, Thou good and gra - cious King.

*T*he triumphant procession began after the disciples obtained the colt (Luke 19:30–34). They were diligent in obeying their Lord's command to procure a donkey, even though it no doubt seemed a trivial request. And still today, obedience is the key to our effective service for God.

The Palm Sunday procession also teaches that our Lord is still leading His people—"bringing many sons to glory" (Heb. 2:10) to our heavenly Jerusalem, "whose architect and builder is God" (Heb. 11:10). Our responsibility is to be His faithful followers, sensitive to His daily leadership.

This favorite Palm Sunday hymn was written in approximately A.D. 820 by Bishop Theodolph of Orleans, France, while he was imprisoned at the monastery of Angers. Theodolph was well known in his day as a poet, pastor, and beloved bishop of Orleans. When Emperor Charlemagne died in 814, the bishop was put in a monastic prison by Charlemagne's son and successor, Louis I the Pious, for allegedly plotting against him.

A well-known legend has long been associated with this hymn. It is believed that a short time before the bishop's death in 821, Louis was visiting in the area where the bishop was imprisoned and by chance passed under his cell. The bishop is said to have been singing and worshiping by himself. When the emperor heard this particular text being sung, he was so moved that he immediately ordered the bishop's release.

The tune's composer, Melchior Teschner, was a German Lutheran pastor. Teschner's melody was considered by J. S. Bach (1685–1750) to be so good that he borrowed it for use in his *St. John's Passion.*

John M. Neale's translation of this Latin hymn has become popular in both Catholic and Protestant English-speaking churches around the world. Neale was a noted nineteenth-century Anglican clergyman and scholar. He left a great legacy to the Christian church in his many translations, especially those of the ancient Greek and Latin hymns of the Eastern church.

---

*As you start the spiritual journey throughout
this special week, begin by breathing this prayer
to your Lord:*

*Teach me your way, O Lord, teach me your way!
Your guiding grace afford—teach me your way!
Help me to walk aright, more by faith, less by sight;
Lead me with heav'nly light,
Teach me your way!*

　　　　　　　　　　　　　　　　—B. Mansell Ramsey

3

Beneath the Cross of Jesus

For the preaching of the cross is to them that perish foolishness; but unto us which are saved it is the power of God.

—1 Corinthians 1:18 (KJV)

Beneath the Cross of Jesus

ELIZABETH C. CLEPHANE, 1830–1869   FREDERICK C. MAKER, 1844–1927

"St. Christopher"

1. Be - neath the cross of Je - sus I fain would take my stand—
2. There lies be - neath its shad - ow, But on the far - ther side,
3. Up - on the cross of Je - sus Mine eyes at times can see
4. I take, O cross, thy shad - ow For my a - bid - ing place.

The sha - dow of a might - y rock With - in a wea - ry land,
The dark - ness of an aw - ful grave That gapes both deep and wide;
The ver - y dy - ing form of One Who suf - fered there for me.
I ask no oth - er sun - shine than The sun - shine of His face;

A home with - in the wil - der - ness, A rest up - on the way
And there be - tween us stands the cross, Two arms out - stretched to save,
And from my smit - ten heart, with tears, These won - ders I con - fess:
Con - tent to let the world go by, To know no gain nor loss,

From the burn - ing of the noon - tide heat And the bur - den of the day.
Like a watch - man set to guard the way From that e - ter - nal grave.
The won - der of His glo - rious love, And my un - wor - thi - ness.
My sin - ful self—my on - ly shame, My glo - ry— all the cross.

Cross of Jesus, cross of sorrow,
Where the blood of Christ was shed;
Perfect Man on thee did suffer,
Perfect God on thee has bled!

—William J. S. Simpson

*T*here is no neutral ground when we face the cross. Either we accept its atoning work and become a new person, or we reject it and remain in our sinful, self-centered state. When we take our stand with Christ and the redemption He accomplished at Calvary, we are compelled to make two profound confessions:

"The wonder of His glorious love" and "my unworthiness."

This hymn of commitment was written by a frail Scottish Presbyterian woman of the nineteenth century. Elizabeth Clephane, despite her physical limitations, was known throughout her charming community of Melrose, Scotland, for her helpfulness and cheery nature. As she visited the sick and shut-ins in her area, she won the name "Sunbeam."

Elizabeth enjoyed writing poems and had several published in a Scottish Presbyterian magazine titled *The Family Treasury*. The majority of her writings, however, appeared anonymously in *Treasury* in 1872, three years after her death at the age of thirty-nine. Of her eight hymns, only one other has endured—"The Ninety and Nine"—made popular by the tune composed for it by Ira D. Sankey.

It is obvious that Elizabeth Clephane, like most Scottish Presbyterians of her day, was an ardent Bible student, for her texts are replete with biblical symbolism and imagery.

- "Mighty Rock" is a reference to Isaiah 32:2.
- "Weary land" is a reference to Psalm 63:1.
- "Home within the wilderness" is a reference to Jeremiah 9:2.
- "Rest upon the way" is a reference to Isaiah 28:12.
- "Noonday heat" is a reference to Isaiah 4:6.
- "Burden of the day" is a reference to Matthew 11:30.

The tune is named "St. Christopher," meaning "bearer of Christ." It was composed for this text by Frederick Charles Maker, one of the outstanding organists in the English nonconformist churches of that day. The text with this music first appeared in the *Bristol Tune Book* in 1881.

"My glory all the cross."
Determine to live the truth of this phrase.

I'm not ashamed to own my Lord,
Nor to defend His cause;
Maintain the honor of His Word,
The glory of His cross.
                                    —*Isaac Watts*

4

Blessed Redeemer

And he died for all, that those who live should no
longer live for themselves but for him who died for
them and was raised again.

—2 Corinthians 5:15

Blessed Redeemer

AVIS B. CHRISTIANSEN, 1895–1985   HARRY DIXON LOES, 1892–1965

1. Up Cal-v'ry's moun-tain, one dread-ful morn, Walked Christ my Sav-ior, wea-ry and worn; Fac-ing for sin-ners death on the cross, That He might save them from end-less loss.
2. "Fa-ther, for-give them!" thus did He pray, E'en while His life-blood flowed fast a-way; Pray-ing for sin-ners while in such woe — No one but Je-sus ev-er loved so.
3. O how I love Him, Sav-ior and Friend! How can my prais-es ev-er find end! Thru years un-num-bered on heav-en's shore, My tongue shall praise Him for-ev-er-more.

CHORUS

Bless-ed Re-deem-er, pre-cious Re-deem-er! Seems now I see Him on Cal-va-ry's tree, Wound-ed and bleed-ing, for sin-ners plead-ing—Blind and un-heed-ing— dy-ing for me!

A Hill with Three Crosses—
One cross where a thief died IN SIN
One cross where a thief died TO SIN
A center cross where a Redeemer died FOR SIN

he composer of this hymn, Harry Dixon Loes, was a popular music teacher at the Moody Bible Institute from 1939 until his death in 1965. He was the author of numerous gospel songs and choruses. One day, while listening to a sermon on the subject of Christ's atonement, Mr. Loes was inspired to compose this tune. He then sent the melody with the suggested title to Mrs. Avis Christiansen, a friend for many years, asking her to write the text. The completed hymn first appeared in *Songs of Redemption* in 1920.

Mrs. Christiansen is one of the most important gospel hymn writers of the twentieth century. She has written hundreds of gospel hymn texts as well as several volumes of published poems. "Everything I've written," she once said, "came from my heart, out of some difficulty or crisis that the Lord brought me through. Although I wasn't good at speaking, I could put anything in poetry." Several of her other well-known gospel songs are "Only Glory By and By," "Blessed Calvary," and "I Know I'll See Jesus Some Day."

Avis was married to E. O. Christiansen, who was affiliated with the Moody Bible Institute in an administrative capacity for nearly forty years. Together they raised two daughters. From 1915 on, Mrs. Christiansen was a faithful member of the Moody Memorial Church of Chicago, Illinois, where she was affectionately known as the "poet laureate." Her former pastor, Dr. Harry A. Ironside, one of the great evangelical leaders and writers of this century, once paid this tribute to Avis Christiansen: "She is a modest, retiring person whom few get to know, beyond the circle of her immediate family and friends. With a very keen apprehension of spiritual realities and a clear understanding of the great truths revealed in the Word of God, her hymns and poems are eminently scriptural and soul-uplifting." A later pastor, Dr. Erwin Lutzer, paid her this tribute: "To know Avis is to become acquainted with a woman who walks closely with her God."

I am living for the moment when before His feet I fall,
And with all the host of heaven own Him Lord and King of all,
Evermore to sing the praises of the Lamb of Calvary,
And to worship and adore Him throughout all eternity.

—Avis B. Christiansen

5

Christ Arose

Now to the King eternal, immortal, invisible, the only
God, be honor and glory for ever and ever. Amen.
—1 Timothy 1:17

Christ Arose

ROBERT LOWRY, 1826–1899

ROBERT LOWRY, 1826–1899

1. Low in the grave He lay– Je - sus, my Sav - ior! Wait - ing the
2. Vain - ly they watch His bed– Je - sus, my Sav - ior! Vain - ly they
3. Death can - not keep his prey– Je - sus, my Sav - ior! He tore the

Refrain
faster

com-ing day– Je - sus, my Lord! Up from the grave He a - rose, With a
seal the dead– Je - sus, my Lord! He a - rose,
bars a - way– Je - sus, my Lord!

might - y tri - umph o'er His foes. He a - rose a Vic - tor from the
He a - rose!

dark do - main, And He lives for - ev - er with His saints to reign. He a-

rit.

rose! He a - rose! Hal - le - lu - jah! Christ a - rose!
He a - rose! He a - rose!

*I*f you and I had been living during the early Christian era, this undoubtedly would have been our greeting to one another, as believers, on an Easter Sunday: "Alleluia, He is risen! Alleluia, He is risen indeed!" For the past century, many congregations celebrating this triumphant day have been inspired anew with the singing of this beloved Easter hymn, written and composed by Robert Lowry in 1874.

Robert Lowry is a highly respected name among early gospel hymn writers. He served for a time as a professor of literature at Bucknell University, pastored several important Baptist churches in the East, and then became the music editor of the Biglow Publishing Company. The quality of Lowry's numerous publications did much to improve the cause of sacred music in this country.

During the Easter season of 1874, while having his devotions one evening, Robert Lowry was impressed with the events surrounding Christ's resurrection, especially with those recorded in Luke 24:6–7 (KJV):

He is not here, but is risen: remember how he spake unto you when he was yet in Galilee, Saying, The Son of man must be delivered into the hands of sinful men, and be crucified, and the third day rise again.

Soon Robert Lowry seated himself at the little pump organ in the parlor of his home. The words and music of "Christ Arose" spontaneously gave expression to the thoughts that had been uppermost in his mind. The hymn was first published in 1875 in the collection *Brightest and Best,* edited by William H. Doane and Robert Lowry.

In addition to "Christ Arose," Lowry has written the words and music for other gospel favorites, such as "Shall We Gather at the River?" and "Nothing But the Blood." He has also supplied the music for these familiar hymns: "We're Marching to Zion," "All the Way My Savior Leads Me," and "I Need Thee Every Hour."

"The Lord is risen indeed!"
He lives to die no more;
He lives His people's cause to plead,
Whose curse and shame He bore.
"The Lord is risen indeed!"
And hell has lost its prey;
And with Him all the ransomed seed
Shall reign in endless day.

—Thomas Kelly

6

Christ the Lord Is Risen Today

"I am the First and the Last. I am the Living One;
I was dead, and behold I am alive for ever and ever!"
—Revelation 1:17–18

Christ the Lord Is Risen Today

CHARLES WESLEY, 1707–1788

Lyra Davidica, 1708

1. Christ the Lord is ris'n to-day. Al - le - lu - ia!
2. Lives a-gain our glo-rious King. Al - le - lu - ia!
3. Love's re-deem-ing work is done. Al - le - lu - ia!
4. Soar we now where Christ has led. Al - le - lu - ia!

Sons of men and an-gels say: Al - le - lu - ia!
Where, O death, is now thy sting? Al - le - lu - ia!
Fought the fight, the bat-tle won. Al - le - lu - ia!
Fol-l'wing our ex-alt-ed Head. Al - le - lu - ia!

Raise your joys and tri-umphs high. Al - le - lu - ia!
Dy-ing once, He all doth save. Al - le - lu - ia!
Death in vain for-bids Him rise. Al - le - lu - ia!
Made like Him, like Him we rise. Al - le - lu - ia!

Sing, ye heav'ns, and earth, re-ply: Al - le - lu - ia!
Where thy vic-to-ry, O grave? Al - le - lu - ia!
Christ has o-pened par-a-dise. Al - le - lu - ia!
Ours the cross, the grave, the skies. Al - le - lu - ia!

What a glorious truth to ponder—Jesus is not the "Great I *Was*" but rather the "Great I *Am!*" He is not only a historical fact but also a present-day, living reality. The whole system of Christianity rests upon the truth that Jesus Christ rose from the grave and is now seated at the Father's right hand as our personal advocate.

"Christ the Lord Is Risen Today" has been one of the church's most popular Easter hymns. Charles Wesley wrote it in 1738, just one year after his "heart-warming" conversion experience at the Aldersgate Hall in London, England. Probably the most frequently sung Easter hymn in the world, it has been called "the Easter hymn par excellence."

The first Wesleyan Chapel in London was a deserted iron foundry, thus becoming known as the Foundry Meeting House. This hymn was written by Charles for the first service in that chapel. It was published in 1739 in Wesley's *Hymns and Sacred Poems* with eleven stanzas. The "alleluias" were not part of the original but were added later by a hymn editor who wanted the hymn sung to a particular tune.

Little is known regarding the origin or the composer of the melody. The music appears to have come from a small tune-book, *Lyra Davidica,* published in 1708 in London. It was a collection of divine songs and hymns, partly translated from High-German and Latin hymns, set to easy and pleasant tunes for more general and private use.

Following his Aldersgate encounter with Christ, Charles began writing numerous hymns on every phase of the Christian experience, about sixty-five hundred in all. It has been stated that the hymns of Charles Wesley clothed Christ in flesh and blood. They gave converts a belief they could easily grasp, embrace with personal faith, and, if necessary, even die for. He is often referred to as the "sweet bard of Methodism."

If all of our eternity is to be realized on this side of the grave, we are hopeless and to be pitied (1 Cor. 15:19). But for the Christian, the Resurrection assures us of God's tomorrow. This anticipation makes it possible to live joyfully today, regardless of life's circumstances.

Christ the Lord is risen on high!
Sing ye heavens and earth reply;
He endured the cross, the grave,
Sinners to redeem and save.
Christ our Lord is risen indeed!
Christ is now the Church's Head;
Loud the song of triumph raise,
Celebrate the Victor's praise.

—Anonymous

7

Crown Him with Many Crowns

His eyes are like blazing fire, and on his head
are many crowns. . . . He is dressed in a robe dipped
in blood, and his name is the Word of God."
—Revelation 19:12–13

Crown Him with Many Crowns

1,2,4 – MATTHEW BRIDGES, 1800–1894 GEORGE J. ELVEY, 1816–1893
3 – GODFREY THRING, 1823–1903

"Diademata"

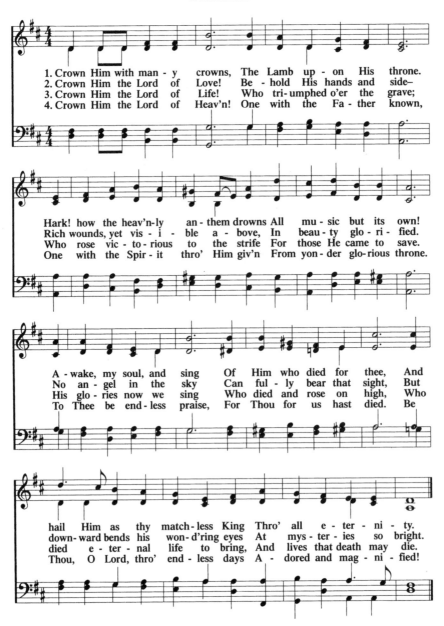

1. Crown Him with man - y crowns, The Lamb up - on His throne.
2. Crown Him the Lord of Love! Be - hold His hands and side–
3. Crown Him the Lord of Life! Who tri-umphed o'er the grave;
4. Crown Him the Lord of Heav'n! One with the Fa - ther known,

Hark! how the heav'n-ly an - them drowns All mu - sic but its own!
Rich wounds, yet vis - i - ble a - bove, In beau - ty glo - ri - fied.
Who rose vic - to - rious to the strife For those He came to save.
One with the Spir - it thro' Him giv'n From yon - der glo-rious throne.

A - wake, my soul, and sing Of Him who died for thee, And
No an - gel in the sky Can ful - ly bear that sight, But
His glo - ries now we sing Who died and rose on high, Who
To Thee be end - less praise, For Thou for us hast died. Be

hail Him as thy match-less King Thro' all e - ter - ni - ty.
down-ward bends his won- d'ring eyes At mys - ter - ies so bright.
died e - ter - nal life to bring, And lives that death may die.
Thou, O Lord, thro' end - less days A - dored and mag - ni - fied!

The Head that once was crowned with thorns
Is crowned with glory now!
A royal diadem adorns
The mighty Victor's brow.

—Thomas Kelly

*T*he One who bore the crown of thorns while on the cross is now crowned with "many crowns" as the reigning monarch of heaven. Each stanza in this hymn text exalts Christ for some specific aspect of His person or ministry:

> Stanza one for His eternal Kingship—
> "thy matchless King thro' all eternity."
> Stanza two for His love demonstrated in redemptive suffering—
> "rich wounds, yet visible above."
> Stanza three for His victorious resurrection and ascension—
> "who triumphed o'er the grave; who rose victorious to the strife."
> Stanza four for the Triune Godhead—
> "One with the Father known; One with the Spirit thro' Him giv'n."

This worshipful text combines the efforts of two distinguished Anglican clergymen, both of whom desired to write a hymn of exaltation to our suffering but victorious Lord. Matthew Bridges's version first appeared in

1851 with six stanzas. Twenty-three years later, Godfrey Thring wrote six additional stanzas, which appeared in his collection *Hymns and Sacred Lyrics*. The hymn's present form includes stanzas one, two, and four by Bridges and the third by Thring.

The tune, "Diademata" (the Greek word for "crowns"), was composed especially for this text by George Elvey, a noted organist at St. George's Chapel in Windsor, where British royalty often attend.

"Be Thou, O Lord, through endless days adored and magnified."

Lamb of God! Thou now art seated
High upon Thy Father's throne;
All Thy gracious work completed,
All Thy mighty vict'ry won.
Every knee in heaven is bending
To the Lamb for sinners slain;
Every voice and harp is swelling,
Worthy is the Lamb to reign.

—James G. Deck

8

Hallelujah, What a Savior!

He was despised and rejected by men, a man of sorrows, and familiar with suffering. . . . He was despised, and we esteemed him not.

—Isaiah 53:3

Therefore God exalted him to the highest place and gave him the name that is above every name, that at the name of Jesus every knee should bow, in heaven and on earth and under the earth, and every tongue confess that Jesus Christ is Lord, to the glory of God the Father.

—Philippians 2:9–11

Hallelujah, What a Savior!

PHILIP P. BLISS, 1838–1876   PHILIP P. BLISS, 1838–1876

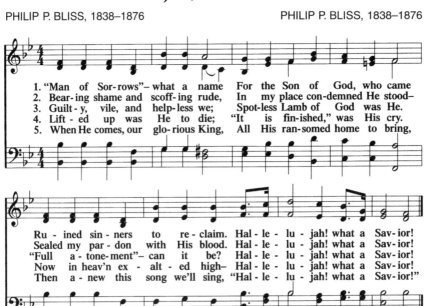

1. "Man of Sor-rows"– what a name   For the Son of God, who came
2. Bear-ing shame and scoff-ing rude,   In my place con-demned He stood–
3. Guilt-y, vile, and help-less we;   Spot-less Lamb of God was He.
4. Lift-ed up was He to die;   "It is fin-ished," was His cry.
5. When He comes, our glo-rious King,   All His ran-somed home to bring,

Ru - ined sin - ners   to   re - claim. Hal-le-lu-jah! what a Sav-ior!
Sealed my par-don   with His blood. Hal-le-lu-jah! what a Sav-ior!
"Full a-tone-ment"– can it   be? Hal-le-lu-jah! what a Sav-ior!
Now in heav'n ex - alt - ed high– Hal-le-lu-jah! what a Sav-ior!
Then a-new this song we'll sing, "Hal-le-lu-jah! what a Sav-ior!"

He Is Lord

Traditional   Traditional

He is Lord!   He is Lord!   He is   ris-en from the dead and He is

Lord!   Ev-'ry knee shall bow, ev-'ry tongue con-fess That Je-sus Christ is Lord.

Jesus Christ, the condescension of divinity
and the exaltation of humanity.

—Phillips Brooks

*T*he word *hallelujah* is basically the same in all languages. It seems as though God gave this word in preparation for the great coronation in heaven. There, His children from every tribe, language, people, and nation are gathered home to voice their eternal hallelujahs (praises) to the victorious Lamb—our Savior forevermore. Hallelujah!

Philip Paul Bliss was highly influential in promoting the growth of early gospel hymnody in this country. A man of commanding stature and an impressive personality for leading congregational singing, Philip Bliss was highly regarded by his colleagues. George Stebbins, also a noted gospel songwriter of that day, paid this tribute to Bliss: "There has been no writer of verse since his time who has shown such a grasp of the fundamental truths of the gospel, or such a gift for putting them into poetic and singable form."

Before his tragic death in a train accident at the age of thirty-eight, Bliss wrote hundreds of gospel songs, often both words and music. His songs were widely used in the D. L. Moody-Ira Sankey evangelistic campaigns throughout the United States and Great Britain. Some of the favorites still sung are "Wonderful Words of Life," "Almost Persuaded," "Jesus Loves Even Me," and "I Gave My Life for Thee." Though Bliss's ministry was brief, his influence continues to the present.

Written one year before his death, "Hallelujah, What a Savior!" is regarded as one of Bliss's finest songs. The first four stanzas simply and clearly present Christ's atoning work. The final stanza, "When He comes our glorious King . . . ," reflects an entirely different mood—joyful and triumphant in its anticipation of the praise that will continue throughout eternity.

- He died that we might live (John 5:24–25).
- He rose again that He might be our eternal Lord (Rom. 14:9).
- He was made sin that we might become righteous (2 Cor. 5:21).
- He became poor that we might become rich (2 Cor. 8:9).

> Hallelujah! What a Savior,
> Hallelujah! What a Friend
> Saving, helping, keeping, loving—
> He is with me to the end.
> —J. Wilbur Chapman

Let your hallelujahs ring loudly and clearly as you ponder the atoning work of Christ and the glorious promise of His return, when "every knee shall bow" and "every tongue confess that Jesus Christ is Lord," to the glory of God the Father.

9

He Lives

I have been crucified with Christ and I no longer live,
but Christ lives in me. The life I live in the body,
I live by faith in the Son of God, who loved me
and gave himself for me.

—Galatians 2:20

He Lives

ALFRED H. ACKLEY, 1887–1960

ALFRED H. ACKLEY, 1887–1960

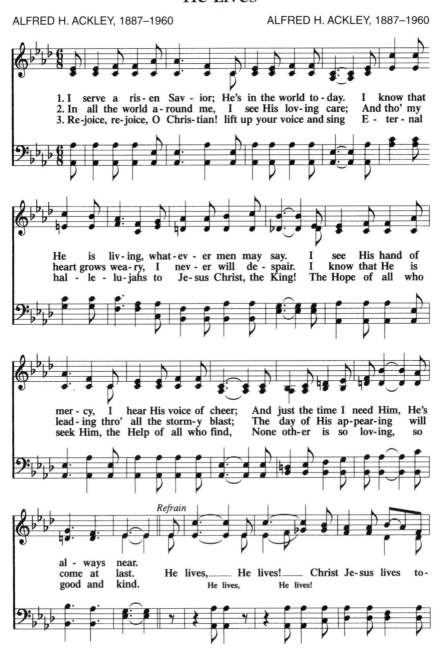

1. I serve a ris-en Sav-ior; He's in the world to-day. I know that
2. In all the world a-round me, I see His lov-ing care; And tho' my
3. Re-joice, re-joice, O Chris-tian! lift up your voice and sing E - ter - nal

He is liv-ing, what-ev-er men may say. I see His hand of
heart grows wea-ry, I nev-er will de - spair. I know that He is
hal - le - lu-jahs to Je-sus Christ, the King! The Hope of all who

mer - cy, I hear His voice of cheer; And just the time I need Him, He's
lead-ing thro' all the storm-y blast; The day of His ap-pear-ing will
seek Him, the Help of all who find, None oth-er is so lov-ing, so

Refrain

al - ways near.
come at last. He lives,___ He lives!___ Christ Je-sus lives to-
good and kind. He lives, He lives!

day! He walks with me and talks with me a - long life's nar - row way. He lives,_____ He lives,_____ sal - va - tion to im - part!

He lives, He lives,

You ask me how I know He lives? He lives with-in my heart!

I know not how that Calvary's cross
a world from sin could free,
I only know its matchless love
has brought new life to me.

—Author Unknown

"Why should I worship a dead Jew?" This challenge was posed by a sincere young Jewish student who had been attending evangelistic meetings conducted by Alfred H. Ackley, author and composer of this favorite gospel hymn.

Ackley's emphatic answer came quickly: "He lives, I tell you. He is not dead, but lives here and now. Jesus Christ is more alive today than ever before. I can prove it by my own experience, as well as the testimony of countless thousands."

The young Jewish student eventually accepted the living Christ as his own personal Savior. Because of the events surrounding this experience, Mr. Ackley read the gospel accounts of the Resurrection with fresh insight. The words "He is risen" suddenly took on new meaning for him. Soon he expressed in song the thrill within his own soul—the indwelling presence of the living Christ. And since its first publication in 1933, "He Lives" continues to inspire Christian congregations with the truth that one of the most compelling proofs of the Resurrection is the daily demonstration by believers that Christ's divine life is now being evidenced in our very bodies.

Alfred Henry Ackley received a thorough education in music, including study in composition, at the Royal Academy of Music in London, England. As a performer, he was recognized as an accomplished cellist. Following graduation from the Westminster Theological Seminary, Ackley was ordained to the Presbyterian ministry.

Even while pastoring churches in Pennsylvania and California, Pastor Ackley maintained a keen interest in the writing of gospel music. He died on July 3, 1960, but during his lifetime, Ackley wrote more than one thousand gospel songs in addition to aiding in the compilation of various hymnals and songbooks for the Rodeheaver Music Company. In recognition of his contribution to sacred music, Alfred Ackley was awarded an honorary Doctor of Sacred Music degree from John Brown University.

But the song for which the Christian church will ever be grateful to Alfred H. Ackley is this one. It thrills our hearts with its triumphant message and silences the skeptic and the scoffer with these words of personal experience:

"You ask me how I know He lives? He lives within my heart!"

Let the bells of Easter toll,
Christ has risen in my soul!
Hear the choir sing and say,
Christ is in my heart today.
Listen while the word is said,
Christ is risen, I am dead!
Voice and bell and organ roll,
Christ is risen in my soul!
—Kenneth Leslie

10

Hosanna, Loud Hosanna

"Hosanna to the Son of David!" "Blessed is he who comes in the name of the Lord!" "Hosanna in the highest!"
—Matthew 21:9

Hosanna, Loud Hosanna

JENNETTE THRELFALL, 1821–1880   Gesangbuch, Würtemberg, 1784

"Ellacombe"

1. "Ho - san - na, loud ho - san - na," The lit - tle chil - dren sang;
2. From Ol - i - vet they fol - lowed 'Mid an ex - ul - tant crowd,
3. "Ho - san - na in the high - est!" That an - cient song we sing,

Thro' pil - lared court and tem - ple The love - ly an - them rang.
The vic - tor palm branch wav - ing, And chant - ing clear and loud.
For Christ is our Re - deem - er, The Lord of heav'n, our King.

To Je - sus, who had blessed them Close fold - ed to His breast,
The Lord of earth and heav - en Rode on in low - ly state,
O may we ev - er praise Him With heart and life and voice,

The chil - dren sang their prais - es, The sim - plest and the best.
Nor scorned that lit - tle chil - dren Should on His bid - ding wait.
And in His bliss - ful pres - ence E - ter - nal - ly re - joice!

O'er all the way, green palms and blossoms gay
Are strewn this day in festal preparation,
When Jesus comes to wipe our tears away;
E'en now the throng to welcome Him prepare.

Join all and sing, His name declare,
Let ev'ry voice resound with acclamation;
Hosanna! Praise to the Lord!
Bless Him who cometh, to bring us salvation!

—Jean-Baptiste Faure

*O*ne can almost hear the chanting crowd and see the children darting about with their palm branches as Christ enters the Holy City.

Jesus was always attuned to the voices of children. He rebuked the religious leaders who, no doubt, were disturbed by these youngsters: "Have you never read, 'From the lips of children and infants you have ordained praise'?" (Matt. 21:16).

Jennette Threlfall, author of this text, captures the scene with Jesus and the children in the first two stanzas of this familiar Palm Sunday hymn. Their singing was "the simplest and the best." The final stanza, however, arouses a sense of victorious praise from all of Christ's followers: "O may we ever praise Him with heart and life and voice."

Jennette Threlfall was orphaned at an early age in England. Later she suffered an accident that made her an invalid for life. Despite her many hardships, she was known for her cheery disposition. This hymn of praise is said to be a reflection of her positive attitude in living for God's glory. Writing spiritual poems, which were usually published anonymously, was her chief pursuit in life. "Hosanna, Loud Hosanna" was first published in 1873 in her volume *Sunshine and Shadow.*

The tune is an anonymous eighteenth-century melody from a collection of German Catholic hymns. A century later it became more widely used in England, where it was titled "Ellacombe" after a village in Devonshire, England.

Many in that first Palm Sunday crowd no doubt cheered Jesus merely as a conquering hero who would hopefully drive out the hated Romans and establish a kingdom of Jewish righteousness. Even today there are many who view Jesus as something other than the sovereign God. The question and the choice still confront every individual: What do you think of Christ? Will you shout "hosanna" or "crucify"?

Discuss the Palm Sunday Scriptures with your family.
Share personal insights about this event. Perhaps
dramatize the setting. Consider how you can offer more
meaningful praise to God throughout this special week.
"Whoso offereth praise glorifieth me"
(Ps. 50:23 KJV).

11

I Know That My Redeemer Liveth

I know that my Redeemer lives, and that in the end
he will stand upon the earth. And after my skin
has been destroyed, yet in my flesh I will see God.
—Job 19:25–26

I Know That My Redeemer Liveth

JESSIE B. POUNDS, 1861–1921   JAMES H. FILLMORE, 1849–1936

stand; I know, I know that life He
stand; I know, I know that life He

giv - eth, That grace and pow'r are in His hand.
giv - eth, That grace and pow'r are in His hand.

I know that my Redeemer lives." This is one of the most sublime expressions of faith ever uttered. It was spoken by an Old Testament patriarch, Job, who had just lost everything in life—possessions, family, and health. Yet in spite of all this, his unequivocal confidence in God remained steadfast: "Though he slay me, yet will I hope in him" (Job 13:15). With the eye of faith, Job also anticipated eternity: "I myself will see him with my own eyes—I, and not another. How my heart yearns within me!" (Job 19:27).

Regardless of the circumstances encountered, we, like Job, must build our lives on a foundation of unwavering faith in God and a bright hope for eternity. Jesus demonstrated this truth in the parable about the wise and foolish builders. When the storms came, the house built on rock stood firm, while the house built on sand crumbled. The storms came to both; the foundations made the difference (Matt. 7:24–27).

The author of this hymn's text, Jessie Brown Pounds, wrote fifty cantata librettos and more than four hundred gospel song texts, including such favorites as "Anywhere with Jesus," "The Way of the Cross Leads Home," and "Beautiful Isle of Somewhere." Jessie Pounds was married to the Rev. John Pounds, long-time pastor of the Central Christian Church in Indianapolis, Indiana, and later a college president in Hiram, Ohio.

The composer of this hymn's music, James H. Fillmore, was a well-known composer, publisher, and singing-school teacher. He wrote and published many anthems, cantatas, and hymn tunes. With his brothers, he founded the Fillmore Music House in Cincinnati, Ohio.

"I Know That My Redeemer Liveth" first appeared in 1893 in an Easter cantata, "Hope's Messenger," by James Fillmore. Several years later it began appearing in church hymnals.

Share your confidence in the living, victorious Christ with another person. Appreciate the difference this confidence makes in life as you face each tomorrow.

> *I know that my Redeemer lives,*
> *What joy this blest assurance gives!*
> *He lives, He lives, who once was dead,*
> *He lives, my everlasting Head!*
> *He lives all glory to His name,*
> *He lives my Savior, still the same;*
> *What joy this blest assurance gives,*
> *I know that my Redeemer lives!*
>
> *—Samuel Medley*

12

In the Cross of Christ I Glory

May I never boast except in the cross of our
Lord Jesus Christ, through which the world has
been crucified to me, and I to the world.

—Galatians 6:14

In the Cross of Christ I Glory

JOHN BOWRING, 1792–1872   ITHAMAR CONKEY, 1815–1867

"Rathbun"

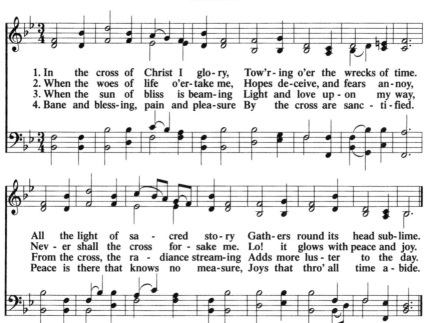

1. In the cross of Christ I glo-ry, Tow'r-ing o'er the wrecks of time.
2. When the woes of life o'er-take me, Hopes de-ceive, and fears an-noy,
3. When the sun of bliss is beam-ing Light and love up-on my way,
4. Bane and bless-ing, pain and plea-sure By the cross are sanc-ti-fied.

All the light of sa-cred sto-ry Gath-ers round its head sub-lime.
Nev-er shall the cross for-sake me. Lo! it glows with peace and joy.
From the cross, the ra-diance stream-ing Adds more lus-ter to the day.
Peace is there that knows no mea-sure, Joys that thro' all time a-bide.

Inscribed upon the cross we see
In shining letters, "God is love";
The Lamb who died upon the tree
Has brought us mercy from above.
The cross! It takes our guilt away,
It holds the fainting spirit up;
It cheers with hope the gloomy day,
And sweetens every bitter cup.

—Thomas Kelly

The cross was a superb triumph over Satan, death, and hell. Never was Christ more a king than when He shouted from the cross: "It is finished." Out of the hideous suffering of Calvary, He has carved His victory and His kingdom.

Throughout church history, the cross has been the most significant symbol of the Christian faith. As many as four hundred different forms or designs of it have been used—among them the usual Latin cross, the Greek cross, and the budded cross. Regardless of the artistic design, the symbol of the cross should always remind us of the price that was paid by the eternal God for our redemption.

"In the Cross of Christ I Glory" is generally considered one of the finest hymns on this subject. It was written in 1825 by one of England's most noted scholars and gifted linguists of the nineteenth century, John Bowring. Bowring could speak twenty-two languages fluently and could communicate in more than one hundred. Before his death at the age of eighty, Bowring also gained fame as a biographer, naturalist, statesman, and philanthropist. He served two terms in the House of Commons and in 1854 was appointed governor of Hong Kong, China. Before his death, he was knighted by the British government for his many accomplishments. Yet despite these many achievements, including thirty-six volumes of published works, John Bowring is best remembered today as the author of this four-stanza hymn, the title of which is inscribed on his tombstone.

It is said that John Bowring had visited Macao on the South Chinese Coast and was much impressed by the sight of a bronze cross towering on the summit of a massive wall of what had formerly been a great cathedral. This cathedral, originally built by the early Portuguese colonists, overlooked the harbor and had been destroyed by a typhoon. Only one wall, which was topped by the huge metal cross, remained. The scene so impressed Bowring that it eventually served as the inspiration for this hymn text.

The melody for this hymn is named "Rathbun." It was composed twenty-four years after Bowring's text by an American organist and choir leader of the Central Baptist Church of Norwich, Connecticut. The composer, Ithamar Conkey, was sorely disappointed and agitated at one Sunday morning service when only one choir member appeared, a faithful soprano named Mrs. Beriah Rathbun. Before the evening service, Conkey composed a new tune for this text and named it after his one faithful choir member.

The message of the cross may be foolish to many, "but unto us which are saved it is the power of God" (1 Cor. 1:18 KJV).

Determine to allow the glory of Christ's cross to be
evident in your life.

13

In the Hour of Trial

No temptation has seized you except what is common to man. And God is faithful; he will not let you be tempted beyond what you can bear. But when you are tempted, he will also provide a way out so that you can stand up under it.

—1 Corinthians 10:13

In the Hour of Trial

JAMES MONTGOMERY, 1771–1854

SPENCER LANE, 1843–1903

"Penitence"

1. In the hour of tri - al, Je - sus, plead for me, Lest, by base de -
2. With for - bid - den plea-sures Would this vain world charm, Or its sor - did
3. Should Thy mer - cy send me Sor - row, toil, and woe; Or should pain at -

ni - al, I de - part from Thee; When Thou seest me wa - ver, With a
trea-sures Spread to work me harm; Bring to my re - mem -brance Sad Geth-
tend me On my path be - low; Grant that I may nev - er Fail Thy

look re - call; Nor for fear or fa - vor Suf - fer me to fall.
sem - a - ne, Or, in dark - er sem-blance, Rug-ged Cal - va - ry.
hand to see; Grant that I may ev - er Cast my care on Thee. A-men.

*C*risis situations are often pivotal for us. Our responses to traumatic times—the loss of a loved one, a change in employment, mistreatment by a trusted friend—will be the foundation stones upon which our lives are built. Maintaining the glow of our first love for God despite difficulties is a major concern.

This fine hymn, first published in 1853 with the title "Prayers on a Pilgrimage," was written by one of England's foremost hymn writers, James Montgomery. The text is based on Peter's denial of his Lord in the courtyard of the high priest (Mark 14:54, 66–72; Luke 22:55–62). The final stanza teaches so well how we should respond when trials come our way: with a desire to know what God is saying through the experience and a willingness to cast our cares on Him.

"In the Hour of Trial" also teaches that believers, like Peter, are capable of rebelling and straying from the fellowship of their Lord. The Bible gives this warning: "If you think you are standing firm, be careful that you don't fall!" (1 Cor. 10:12). The antidote to sin's allurements is keeping our minds centered on Christ and His redemptive work. Our fellowship with God, like that of Peter, can be restored when we return to Him in brokenness and true humility. Peter's remorse was the start of his spiritual greatness.

James Montgomery, the author of this text, was for thirty-one years the editor of an influential English newspaper, *The Sheffield Iris*. He was an ardent champion of various humanitarian causes, including the abolition of slavery. He was also a strong supporter of foreign missions and the British Bible Society. James Montgomery was the author of approximately four hundred hymns, including "Angels from the Realms of Glory," "Prayer Is the Soul's Sincere Desire," and "Stand up and Bless the Lord."

The tune, "Penitence," originally intended for another text, was composed in 1875 by Spencer Lane, a well-known music teacher in New York City.

Share with another believer who has strayed from God that he or she can have a new beginning with Christ. God is available to help in every situation.

Just when I need Him Jesus is near,
just when I falter, just when I fear;
Ready to help me, ready to cheer,
just when I need Him most.

—William C. Poole

14

Jesus Paid It All

"Come now, let us reason together," says the LORD.
"Though your sins are like scarlet, they shall be
as white as snow; though they are red as crimson,
they shall be like wool."

—Isaiah 1:18

Jesus Paid It All

ELVINA M. HALL, 1820–1889   JOHN T. GRAPE, 1835–1915

1. I hear the Sav - ior say: "Thy strength in - deed is small.
2. Lord, now in - deed I find Thy pow'r, and Thine a - lone,
3. For noth - ing good have I Where - by Thy grace to claim;
4. And when be - fore the throne I stand in Him com - plete,

Child of weak - ness, watch and pray. Find in Me thine All in
Can change the lep - er's spots, And melt the heart of
I'll wash my gar - ments white In the blood of Cal - v'ry's
"Je - sus died my soul to save," My lips shall still re -

Refrain

All."
stone.   Je - sus paid it all; All to Him I owe.
Lamb.
peat.

Sin had left a crim - son stain; He washed it white as snow.

No blood, no altar now, the sacrifice is o'er;
No flame, no smoke ascends on high,
    the Lamb is slain no more;
But richer blood has flowed from nobler veins,
To purge the soul from guilt,
    and cleanse the vilest stains.

                    —Horatius Bonar

How important and necessary it is that we learn the truth of this hymn—there is nothing we can do to merit salvation. God has done it all. The Scriptures declare that our finest works are but as filthy rags in His sight (Isaiah 64:6). St. Augustine, an important early church father, stated this same truth in the fifth century: "The sufficiency of my merit is to know that my merit is not sufficient."

This hymn text was written by a laywoman named Elvina Hall one Sunday morning while she was seated in the choir loft of the Monument Street Methodist Church in Baltimore, Maryland. She was supposed to be listening to the sermon being delivered by her pastor, the Rev. George Schrick. One can imagine, however, Elvina Hall saying something like this following the service.

> Pastor Schrick, I must confess that I wasn't listening too closely to your message this morning because, you see, once you started preaching about how we can really

know God's love and forgiveness, I began thinking about
all that Christ has already done to provide our salvation.
Then these words came to me, and I just had to get them
down on paper. And the only paper I could find at the
time was the flyleaf of this hymnal. So I scribbled the
words on that.

The pastor recalled that the church organist, John Grape, had only
just recently given him a copy of a new tune that he had composed and
titled "All to Christ I Owe." To the amazement of all, John Grape's tune fit
perfectly with the words that Elvina Hall had scribbled on the flyleaf
page of the hymnal.

Since its first published appearance in 1874, the hymn has been
widely used in church services, teaching the truth that no one is beyond
God's redeeming grace—it "can change the leper's spots and melt the
heart of stone."

Not what these hands have done
　Can save this guilty soul;
Not what this toiling flesh has borne
　Can make my spirit whole.
Thy work alone, O Christ,
　Can ease this weight of sin;
Thy blood alone, O Lamb of God,
　Can give me peace within.
I bless the Christ of God,
　I rest on love divine;
And with unfalt'ring lip and heart,
　I call this Savior mine.
　　　　　　　—Horatius Bonar

15

Lead Me to Calvary

Consider him who endured such opposition from sinful men, so that you will not grow weary and lose heart.

—Hebrews 12:3

Lead Me to Calvary

JENNIE E. HUSSEY, 1874–1958

WILLIAM J. KIRKPATRICK, 1838–1921

"Duncannon"

1. King of my life I crown Thee now; Thine shall the glo - ry be.
2. Show me the tomb where Thou wast laid, Ten - der - ly mourned and wept;
3. Let me, like Mar - y, thro' the gloom Come with a gift to Thee.
4. May I be will - ing, Lord, to bear Dai - ly my cross for Thee—

Lest I for-get Thy thorn-crowned brow, Lead me to Cal - va - ry.
An - gels in robes of light ar - rayed Guard-ed Thee whilst Thou slept.
Show to me now the emp - ty tomb; Lead me to Cal - va - ry.
E - ven Thy cup of grief to share. Thou hast borne all for me.

Refrain

Lest I for-get Geth - sem - a- ne, Lest I for- get Thine ag - o- ny,

Lest I for-get Thy love for me, Lead me to Cal - va - ry.

The cross of Christ is either a blessing or a curse, depending on our response to it. Either it leads to our eternal redemption or it condemns us to eternal damnation. The choice is demonstrated by the two thieves who hung on either side of the Savior. One responded and received divine mercy; the other rebelled his way into hell.

As God's people, we should live daily with an awareness of Christ's cross. We should review its scenes of suffering as well as revel in its triumph. But simply knowing about Christ's atoning work is not enough. We must personally appropriate it. We must say with conviction, "It was for me that He suffered, died, and rose again!"

"Lead Me to Calvary" first appeared in *New Songs of Praise and Power,* number 3, 1921. Jennie Hussey, the author of the text, was a Quaker whose life was filled with hardship. She cared for an invalid sister and later, after suffering a disease, used a wheelchair for a number of years.

Yet Jennie was known for her cheerful and courageous attitude. The final stanza of this hymn is thought to be an expression of her own submissiveness to her Lord: "May I be willing, Lord, to bear daily my cross for Thee. . . ."

William J. Kirkpatrick, the composer of this music, was a successful furniture dealer in Philadelphia before devoting his time fully to gospel music. He wrote the music for Jennie Hussey's text shortly before his death and named the tune "Duncannon" for his birthplace in Pennsylvania. Kirkpatrick was the compiler of more than one hundred music books and the composer of many other gospel song favorites, including "'Tis

So Sweet to Trust in Jesus," "He Hideth My Soul," "Jesus Saves,"
"Redeemed," and "Oh, to Be Like Thee."

May this hymn by an invalid woman awaken our appreciation for
Christ's suffering and death on Calvary's cross and prepare us for the
glorious celebration of the empty tomb on Easter morning.

Hope we not in this life only, Christ has made it plain
None who sleep in Him shall perish, and our faith
   is not in vain.
Not in vain our glad hosannas since we follow
   where He led;
Not in vain our Easter anthem: "Christ has risen
   from the dead!"

                                 —Anonymous

16

Let Us Break Bread Together

And he took bread, gave thanks and broke it,
and gave it to them, saying, "This is my body
given for you; do this in remembrance of me."

—Luke 22:19

Let Us Break Bread Together

American Folk Hymn

American Folk Melody

1. Let us break bread to - geth-er on our knees;_____
2. Let us drink the cup to - geth-er on our knees;_____
3. Let us praise God to - geth-er on our knees;_____

knees, on our knees;

Let us break bread to - geth-er on our knees;_____
Let us drink the cup to - geth-er on our knees;_____
Let us praise God to - geth-er on our knees;_____

knees, on our knees;

Refrain

When I fall on my knees with my face to the ris - ing sun,

O Lord, have mer-cy on me._____

me, on me.

According to Thy gracious word, in meek humility,
This will I do, my dying Lord: I will remember Thee.
Thy body, broken for my sake, my bread from heav'n
shall be;
Thy testamental cup I take, and thus remember Thee.

—James Montgomery

*I*n His sovereign wisdom, our Lord knew that through the centuries His followers would need a continual reminder of the essential truths of their faith—the sacrificial death, the triumphant resurrection, and the victorious return of Christ. At the Last Supper, Christ introduced to His disciples the signs of the new covenant—His broken body and shed blood—symbolized by the bread and the cup. With this supper as the model, He then gave instruction that this feast of remembrance should occur regularly in our worship of Him until He comes. After that, the feast will culminate in heaven with the saints of the ages in the wedding supper of the Lamb (Rev. 19:7, 9).

The Lord's Supper also teaches an important truth concerning the corporate relationship that should exist between fellow believers. The local church has been described as a laboratory where believers learn to love one another regardless of color, nationality, or financial status. Our common heavenly citizenship is the one dominant tie that binds our hearts together. This bond of fellowship should result in God's family members learning to care, honor, and serve one another in love. We should treat others with the same tender compassion that we have received from God Himself.

As with most folk music, neither the author nor the date of this song's composition is known. First published by a black poet, James Weldon Johnson, in 1927, it is one of the few spirituals referring to the Communion service. Some researchers of black slave music have suggested that this folk hymn might have been used by African Americans in secret meetings. In the colony of Virginia before the Civil War, such religious gatherings were prohibited.

Remembering Christ's death should lead to greater nobleness of life. Anticipating His return should lead to greater purity of life.

Here, O my Lord, I see Thee face to face;
Here would I touch and handle things unseen;
Here grasp with firmer hand eternal grace;
And all my weariness upon Thee lean.
Here would I feed upon the bread of God,
Here drink with Thee the royal wine of heav'n;
Here would I lay aside each earthly load,
Here taste afresh the calm of sin forgiv'n.

—Horatius Bonar

17

Majestic Sweetness Sits Enthroned

But we see Jesus, who was made a little lower than the angels, now crowned with glory and honor because he suffered death, so that by the grace of God he might taste death for everyone.

—Hebrews 2:9

Majestic Sweetness Sits Enthroned

SAMUEL STENNETT, 1727–1795
THOMAS HASTINGS, 1784–1872

"Ortonville"

1. Ma - jes - tic sweet - ness sits en - throned Up - on the
2. No mor - tal can with Him com - pare A - mong the
3. He saw me plunged in deep dis - tress And flew to
4. To Him I owe my life and breath And all the

Sav - ior's brow; His head with ra - diant glo - ries crowned, His
sons of men; Fair - er is He than all the fair Who
my re - lief; For me He bore the shame - ful cross And
joys I have; He makes me tri - umph o - ver death And

lips with grace o'er - flow, His lips with grace o'er - flow.
fill the heav'n - ly train, Who fill the heav'n - ly train.
car - ried all my grief, And car - ried all my grief.
saves me from the grave, And saves me from the grave.

O Head, once filled with bruises,
Oppressed with pain and scorn,
O'erwhelmed with sore abuses,
Mocked with a crown of thorns!
O Head, to death once wounded
In shame upon the tree,
In glory now surrounded
With brightest majesty!

—Paul Gerhardt

The dominant theme of this beautifully expressed text is the adoration of Jesus Christ. The words are based on the descriptive passage found in the Song of Solomon 5:10–16. Here the awaiting maiden, anticipating the return of her lover, describes him: "Chief among ten thousand," "head of pure gold," "body like polished ivory," and "altogether lovely."

The hymn originally had nine stanzas and was titled "The Chief Among Ten Thousand" or "The Excellencies of Christ." It first appeared in John Rippon's famous Baptist collection, *A Selection of Hymns from the Best of Authors,* published in 1787.

The Bible often refers to believers as the bride of Christ. We, too, are awaiting the return of our lover, the One who is "fairer than all the fair . . . and saves me from the grave."

The author, Samuel Stennett, was a well-known Baptist pastor in London, England, and was regarded as one of the outstanding evangelical preachers of his day. Dr. Stennett was also an influential writer on numerous theological subjects as well as the author of thirty-nine hymns, including the still popular "On Jordan's Stormy Banks."

The popularity of this hymn text was enhanced by the tune composed for it in 1837 by the talented American church musician, Thomas Hastings. He is credited with being one of the most influential church musicians of the nineteenth century. His efforts raised the standard of sacred music in this country. Despite a serious eye affliction, he composed more than one thousand hymn tunes as well as more than six hundred hymn texts. Several of his hymn tunes still in use include "Rock of Ages," "From Every Stormy Wind That Blows," and "Come, Ye Disconsolate."

Express your feelings of love and adoration to
your heavenly bridegroom; anticipate actually seeing
Him some day soon.

Then to the Lamb once slain
Be glory, praise and power,
Who died and lives again,
Who liveth evermore;
Who loved us, cleansed us by His blood,
And made us kings and priests to God!
—Horatius Bonar

18

My Jesus, I Love Thee

This is love: not that we loved God, but that he loved us and sent his Son as an atoning sacrifice for our sins. We love because he first loved us.

—1 John 4:10,19

My Jesus, I Love Thee

WILLIAM R. FEATHERSTON, 1846–1873   ADONIRAM J. GORDON, 1836–1895

"Gordon"

1. My Je - sus, I love Thee; I know Thou art mine. For Thee all the
2. I love Thee be - cause Thou hast first lov - ed me, And pur-chased my
3. I will love Thee in life, I will love Thee in death, And praise Thee as
4. In man-sions of glo - ry and end - less de-light, I'll ev - er a-

fol - lies of sin I re - sign. My gra - cious Re - deem - er, my
par - don on Cal - va - ry's tree. I love Thee for wear - ing the
long as Thou lend - est me breath, And say when the death - dew lies
dore Thee in heav - en so bright. I'll sing with the glit - ter-ing

Sav - ior art Thou. If ev - er I loved Thee, my Je - sus, 'tis now.
thorns on Thy brow. If ev - er I loved Thee, my Je - sus, 'tis now.
cold on my brow, "If ev - er I loved Thee, my Je - sus, 'tis now."
crown on my brow, "If ev - er I loved Thee, my Je - sus, 'tis now."

Blest be Thy love, dear Lord,
　　that taught us this sweet way,
Only to love Thee for Thyself,
　　and for that love obey.
　　　　　　　　　　　—Author Unknown

*I*f we are to love and worship God acceptably, we must begin by recognizing who He is. Our concept of Him will continue to expand as we grow in grace and in our knowledge of the Lord (2 Peter 3:18). In a child's earliest years, devotion to his or her parents is based mainly on the parents' ability to fulfill basic needs. By the time children reach young adulthood, however, they should be developing a deep love for their parents simply for who they are. Children should also be experiencing a growing desire to please their parents. Similarly, we must mature spiritually in our appreciation of God and in our love relationship with Him. We must worship our Lord not only for what He has done and will do in our lives, but above all for who He is—for His being, character, and works.

The spiritual depth of this hymn is all the more remarkable since it was written by a teenager. William Ralph Featherston of Montreal, Canada, is thought to have written these lines of gratitude to Christ at the time of his conversion experience when only sixteen. It is believed he sent a copy of his poem to an aunt in Los Angeles, and somehow the text appeared anonymously in print in an English hymnal, *The London Book,* in 1864.

Several years later, a well-known American Baptist pastor, Dr. A. J. Gordon, discovered the anonymous hymn in the English hymnal and decided to compose a better melody for it. With its new tune, the hymn has since been included in nearly every evangelical hymnal and has been sung frequently by believers everywhere during hushed moments of rededication to God.

The Scriptures teach that loving God acceptably is never an easy matter. Jesus said that love of God includes our hearts, our souls, our minds, and a selfless love for our neighbors (Matt. 22:37–39). The apostle John further reminds us that we are not to "love with words or tongue but with actions and in truth" (1 John 3:18).

As you reflect on the cost of your eternal salvation, whisper this musical prayer to the Lord: "If ever I loved Thee, my Jesus, 'tis now."

———————————

My God, I love Thee, not because I hope for heaven thereby,
Nor yet because those who love Thee not must die eternally.
E'en so I love Thee, and will love and in Thy praise will sing—
Solely because Thou art my God, and my eternal King!
                                    — "My Eternal King" by Francis Xavier
                                    Translated by Edward Caswall

19

O Sacred Head, Now Wounded

And when they had platted a crown of thorns,
they put it upon his head, and a reed in his
right hand: and they bowed the knee before him,
and mocked him, saying, Hail, King of the Jews!
And they spit upon him, and took the reed,
and smote him on the head.

—Matthew 27:29–30 (KJV)

O Sacred Head, Now Wounded

Attr. BERNARD OF CLAIRVAUX, 1091–1153
Trans. PAUL GERHARDT, 1607–1676
Trans. JAMES W. ALEXANDER, 1804–1859

HANS LEO HASSLER, 1564–1612
Har. JOHANN SEBASTIAN BACH,
1685–1750

"Passion Chorale"

1. O sa - cred Head, now wound-ed, With grief and shame weighed down,
2. What Thou, my Lord, hast suf - fered Was all for sin - ners' gain.
3. What lan-guage shall I bor - row To thank Thee, dear - est Friend,

Now scorn-ful - ly sur - round - ed With thorns, Thine on - ly crown;
Mine, mine was the trans - gres - sion, But Thine the dead - ly pain.
For this Thy dy - ing sor - row, Thy pit - y with - out end?

O sa - cred Head, what glo - ry, What bliss till now was Thine!
Lo, here I fall, my Sav - ior! 'Tis I de - serve Thy place.
O make me Thine for - ev - er; And, should I faint - ing be,

Yet, tho' de - spised and gor - y, I joy to call Thee mine.
Look on me with Thy fa - vor; And grant to me Thy grace.
Lord, let me nev - er, nev - er Out - live my love to Thee.

O mysterious condescending! O abandonment sublime!
Very God Himself is bearing all the suffering of time!
—William J. S. Simpson

The text of this deeply moving hymn is thought to have its roots in twelfth-century monastic life. It has long been attributed to Saint Bernard, abbot of the monastery of Clairvaux, France. It is still the most universally used hymn during the Lenten season.

It is generally agreed that Bernard of Clairvaux became one of the finest and most influential church leaders of the Middle Ages. He is said to have represented the best of monastic life in his time. The emphasis of his ministry was a life of holiness, simplicity, devotion, prayer, preaching, and ministering to the physical and spiritual needs of others.

"O Sacred Head, Now Wounded" is taken from a lengthy medieval poem that consisted of seven parts, each part addressing various members of Christ's body as He suffered on the cross: His feet, knees, hands, side, breast, heart, and face. This hymn text is from the seventh portion of the poem and was originally titled "Salve Caput Cruentatum."

The stanzas of the hymn were translated into German in the seventeenth century by Paul Gerhardt, one of Germany's foremost hymn writers. Two centuries later, the hymn was translated into English by Dr. James Alexander, an American scholar and professor of church history at Princeton Seminary.

This classic hymn has shown in three tongues—Latin, German and English—and in three confessions—Roman, Lutheran and Reformed—with equal effect, the dying love of our Savior and our boundless indebtedness to Him.
—Philip Schaff

The tune, "Passion Chorale," was originally a German love song in Hans Leo Hassler's collection of 1601. Hassler is generally considered to be one of the finest late-Renaissance German composers of both secular and sacred music. The harmonization of this tune is by the German master-composer, Johann Sebastian Bach, undoubtedly one of the greatest church musicians in history. It would appear that Bach was especially fond of this melody, since he used the chorale five times throughout his well-known *St. Matthew Passion,* which was composed in 1729.

God has preserved this exceptional hymn, which has through the centuries led Christians to more ardent worship of His Son.

Ponder anew your suffering Savior. Breathe this prayer of commitment— "Lord, let me never, never outlive my love to Thee."

20

The Strife Is O'er

O death, where is thy sting? O grave, where is thy victory? But thanks be to God, which giveth us the victory through our Lord Jesus Christ.
—1 Corinthians 15:55, 57 (KJV)

The Strife Is O'er

Latin Hymn, c. 1695
Trans. FRANCIS POTT, 1832–1909

GIOVANNI P. DA PALESTRINA, c. 1525–1594
Adapted WILLIAM H. MONK, 1823–1889

"Victory"

Al - le - lu - ia! Al - le - lu - ia! Al - le - lu - ia!

Organ

1. The strife is o'er— the bat - tle done, The vic - to - ry of life is
2. The pow'rs of death have done their worst, But Christ their le - gions hath dis -
3. The three sad days have quick-ly sped, He ris - es glo-rious from the
4. He closed the yawn-ing gates of hell, The bars from heav'n's high por - tals
5. Lord, by the stripes which wound-ed Thee, From death's dread sting Thy serv- ants

won; The song of tri - umph has be - gun: Al - le - lu - ia!
persed; Let shouts of ho - ly joy out-burst: Al - le - lu - ia!
dead; All glo- ry to our ris - en Head! Al - le - lu - ia!
fell; Let hymns of praise His tri - umphs tell: Al - le - lu - ia!
free, That we may live and sing to Thee: Al - le - lu - ia!

The atoning work is done,
The Victim's blood is shed;
And Jesus now has gone
His people's cause to plead.
He stands in heaven, their great High Priest,
And bears their names upon His breast.

—Thomas Kelly

The battle is over—the victory of life is won—Christ has triumphed over death! This message dispels our fears and gives us the sure hope that, because He lives, we also shall live (John 14:19). Alleluia!

This inspiring hymn first appeared anonymously in a Jesuit collection, *Symphonia Sirenum,* published in Cologne, Germany, in 1695. The joyous music of the great sixteenth-century Catholic composer, Palestrina, no doubt contributes to the enduring popularity of the hymn.

Giovanni Palestrina came to Rome in 1551 to become organist and director of the Julian Choir, the performing choir at St. Peter's Church in the Vatican. His beautiful *a cappella* style of choral writing has made the sixteenth century known as the "golden age of choral polyphony."

Among Palestrina's many works are approximately one hundred masses, two hundred motets, hymns, offertories, and other liturgical works.

It was more than 150 years after its writing, however, before this hymn was used by English-speaking churches. In 1859 Francis Pott, an Anglican minister, made the translation. Pastor Pott always maintained a strong interest in hymnology throughout his ministry. He was a member of the original committee that prepared the prestigious Anglican hymnal, *Hymns Ancient and Modern* (1861).

The music for the hymn was arranged by Dr. William H. Monk for inclusion in *Hymns Ancient and Modern*. Monk was the music editor of this hymnal, considered by hymnologists to be one of the most important ever published.

It is interesting to note the interplay between the stated facts of Christ's resurrection contained in the first half of each stanza and the personal response to these truths expressed in the last half of each verse, concluding with the jubilant "Alleluia!" (praise the Lord).

---

*Allow your soul to vibrate with the resounding
"Alleluias" as you anticipate Easter morning
and the celebration of the empty tomb.*

*Jesus lives! thy terror now can, O death,
    no more appall us;
Jesus lives! by this we know thou, O grave,
    cannot enthrall us.*

*—Christian Furchtegott Gellert
Translated by Frances Elizabeth Cox*

21

There Is a Fountain

But now in Christ Jesus you who once were far away
have been brought near through the blood of Christ.
—Ephesians 2:13

There Is a Fountain

WILLIAM COWPER, 1731–1800   American Folk Melody

1. There is a foun-tain filled with blood Drawn from Im-man-uel's veins;
2. The dy-ing thief re-joiced to see That foun-tain in his day;
3. Dear dy-ing Lamb, Thy pre-cious blood Shall nev-er lose its pow'r
4. E'er since, by faith, I saw the stream Thy flow-ing wounds sup-ply,
5. When this poor lisp-ing, stam-m'ring tongue Lies si-lent in the grave,

And sin-ners, plunged be-neath that flood, Lose all their guilt-y stains,
And there may I, tho' vile as he, Wash all my sins a-way,
Till all the ran-somed Church of God Be saved, to sin no more;
Re-deem-ing love has been my theme And shall be till I die,
Then in a no-bler, sweet-er song I'll sing Thy pow'r to save,

Lose all their guilt-y stains, Lose all their guilt-y stains.
Wash all my sins a-way, Wash all my sins a-way.
Be saved, to sin no more; Be saved, to sin no more;
And shall be till I die, And shall be till I die.
I'll sing Thy pow'r to save, I'll sing Thy pow'r to save.

And sin-ners, plunged be-neath that flood, Lose all their guilt-y stains.
And there may I, tho' vile as he, Wash all my sins a-way,
Till all the ran-somed Church of God Be saved, to sin no more.
Re-deem-ing love has been my theme And shall be till I die.
Then in a no-bler, sweet-er song I'll sing Thy pow'r to save.

Lord, I believe Thy precious blood,
Which at the mercy seat of God,
Forever doth for sinners plead,
For me, e'en for my soul was shed.
—Translated by John Wesley

*W*illiam Cowper (pronounced "Kooper") is viewed by some as one of the finest of all English writers. Several of his best known secular works include a translation of Homer, a widely acclaimed volume of poems titled *The Task,* and his most famous literary poem, "John Gilpin," a happy and mirthful narrative.

Cowper, however, experienced great turmoil. At an early age, he was directed by his father to study law. But when his studies were completed, he so dreaded the prospect of appearing for his final examination before the bar that he suffered a mental breakdown and attempted suicide. Later he was placed in an asylum for eighteen months. During detention, he read the passage in Romans 3:25: Jesus Christ is "set forth to be a propitiation through faith in his blood, to declare his righteousness for the remission of sins that are past, through the forbearance of God" (KJV). Through his reading of the Bible, Cowper soon developed a personal relationship with Christ and sensed a forgiveness of sin.

A short time later, Cowper was invited to move to Olney, England, where John Newton (author of "Amazing Grace") pastored the Anglican parish church. It was here for nearly two decades that Newton and Cowper shared a close personal friendship. In 1779 their combined talents produced the famous *Olney Hymns* hymnal, one of the most important single contributions made to the field of evangelical hymnody. In this ambitious collection of 349 hymns, sixty-seven were written by Cowper, the remainder by Newton. The hymnal contains many of our finest hymns, including this one, which emphasizes the cleansing from sin by the atoning sacrifice of Christ.

"There Is a Fountain" was originally titled "Peace for the Fountain Opened." The hymn with its vivid imagery is based on the Old Testament text, Zechariah 13:1: "In that day there shall be a fountain opened to the house of David and to the inhabitants of Jerusalem for sin and for uncleanness" (KJV).

The tune for this text is borrowed from an American folk melody, probably one of the typical tunes used in the camp meetings of the early nineteenth century.

Throughout his life, Cowper continued to be plagued with periodic melancholia. Despite his emotional frailties, William Cowper was endowed by God with extraordinary literary talents that for two centuries have enriched the lives of Christians.

Carry the joy of "redeeming love" as your day's theme.

22

There Is a Green Hill Far Away

For God was pleased to have all his fullness dwell
in him, and through him to reconcile to
himself all things, whether things on earth
or things in heaven, by making peace through
his blood, shed on the cross.

—Colossians 1:19–20

There Is a Green Hill Far Away

CECIL F. ALEXANDER, 1818–1895 · GEORGE C. STEBBINS, 1846–1945

1. There is a green hill far a - way, With - out a cit - y wall,
2. We may not know, we can - not tell What pains He had to bear;
3. He died that we might be for-giv'n, He died to make us good,
4. There was no oth - er good e - nough To pay the price of sin;

Where the dear Lord was cru - ci - fied, Who died to save us all.
But we be - lieve it was for us He hung and suf - fered there.
That we might go at last to heav'n, Saved by His pre - cious blood.
He on - ly could un - lock the gate Of heav'n and let us in.

CHORUS

O dear - ly, dear - ly has He loved! And we must love Him too,

And trust in His re - deem-ing blood, And try His works to do.

*I*t is difficult to fully understand the depth of suffering Christ endured at Calvary for our redemption. Mrs. Cecil Alexander, one of England's finest hymn writers, tried to explain to her Sunday school class the phrase from the Apostles' Creed, "suffered under Pontius Pilate, was crucified, dead and buried." She felt inadequate to the task. She had always believed that one of the most effective ways to teach sound spiritual truths to children is through the use of appropriate hymns. She decided, therefore, to put the details of Christ's suffering and death on the cross into a simply worded but appealing song that could be easily understood by the children in her class. Although the hymn's direct style of wording and clearly expressed thoughts were originally intended for youth, it had an immediate appeal to adults as well.

The lilting melody was composed for the text in 1878 by George C. Stebbins. The hymn became widely used in the Moody-Sankey evangelistic campaigns and has been heard in church services since then.

Mrs. Alexander's life was even more beautiful than her writing. Before her marriage, she had been active in the Sunday school movement. That interest never diminished. Almost all of her four hundred poems and hymns were prompted by her love of children and her interest in their spiritual instruction.

After her marriage at the age of thirty-two to William Alexander, archbishop and primate of the Anglican church for all of Ireland, she became deeply involved in parish duties and charity work. Her husband said of her, "From one poor home to another she went. Christ was ever with her, and all felt her influence."

George C. Stebbins, composer of the melody, is well known in the field of American gospel music. He was a close associate of D. L. Moody and Ira Sankey in their evangelistic ministry. He also worked with such leading evangelists as George F. Pentecost and Major D. W. Whittle. Other hymns by George Stebbins include "Have Thine Own Way, Lord!" "Saved by Grace," and "Ye Must Be Born Again."

We should be thankful to our Lord that through the years each generation can learn the true meaning of Christ's redemptive love from a choice hymn like this.

Express your gratitude for Christ's "redeeming blood."
Let the truth of His great love motivate you to
"try His works to do."

Amazing love! How can it be
That Thou, my God, shouldst die for me?
—Charles Wesley

23

'Tis Midnight; and on Olive's Brow

When they had sung a hymn, they went out
to the Mount of Olives.

—Matthew 26:30

'Tis Midnight; and on Olive's Brow

WILLIAM B. TAPPAN, 1794–1849   WILLIAM B. BRADBURY, 1816–1868

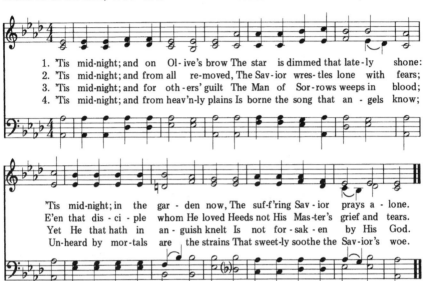

1. 'Tis mid-night; and on Ol- ive's brow The star is dimmed that late-ly shone:
2. 'Tis mid-night; and from all re-moved, The Sav-ior wres- tles lone with fears;
3. 'Tis mid-night; and for oth-ers' guilt The Man of Sor-rows weeps in blood;
4. 'Tis mid-night; and from heav'n-ly plains Is borne the song that an - gels know;

'Tis mid-night; in the gar - den now, The suf-f'ring Sav - ior prays a - lone.
E'en that dis - ci - ple whom He loved Heeds not His Mas-ter's grief and tears.
Yet He that hath in an - guish knelt Is not for - sak - en by His God.
Un-heard by mor-tals are the strains That sweet-ly soothe the Sav-ior's woe.

Go to dark Gethsemane,
    all who feel the tempter's pow'r;
Your Redeemer's conflict see,
    watch with Him one bitter hour.
Turn not from His griefs away—
    learn of Jesus Christ to pray.
Follow to the judgment hall,
    view the Lord of life arraigned.
O the wormwood and the gall!
    O the pangs His soul sustained!
Shun not suff'ring, shame, or loss—
    learn of Him to bear the cross.
Calv'ry's mournful mountain climb;
    there, adoring at His feet,
Mark the miracle of time,
    God's own sacrifice complete.
"It is finished!" hear Him cry—
    learn of Jesus Christ to die.

                    —James Montgomery

*D*ealing with Jesus' agony in the Garden of Gethsemane, this hymn was originally titled "Gethsemane." The short, twelve-measure, descriptive text depicts vividly the anguishing Savior as He prays alone.

The hymn's text was written by William B. Tappan, a Congregational minister in Massachusetts. Before becoming a licensed minister of the

Congregational denomination in 1840, Tappan was active in promoting the Sunday school movement throughout the country. He was appointed superintendent of the American Sunday School Union, a position he held until his death in 1849. Tappan wrote several volumes of poems, in which eight hymns were included. "Gethsemane" first appeared in one of his published collections in 1822.

William B. Bradbury, composer of the music, was a prominent nineteenth-century gospel musician, who taught singing classes throughout the eastern states and conducted musical conventions. He composed and edited fifty-nine collections of sacred and secular music. He was also the manufacturer of the popular Bradbury pianos. William Bradbury is the composer of such other timeless hymns as "Jesus Loves Me," "He Leadeth Me," "The Solid Rock," "Sweet Hour of Prayer," and "Just As I Am."

"'Tis Midnight; and on Olive's Brow" first appeared with Bradbury's tune in a hymnal, *The Shawn,* which was compiled by Bradbury and George F. Root and published in 1853.

When Jesus faced the most crucial crisis of His earthly life, He spent time alone in earnest communion with His heavenly Father. And despite His own desires, His prayer contained those all-important words: "Not my will but Yours be done."

Breathe this earnest prayer to your Lord even now:

Teach me to pray, Lord, teach me to pray;
This is my heartcry day unto day;
I long to know Thy will and Thy way;
Teach me to pray, Lord, teach me to pray.
—Albert S. Reitz

24

Were You There?

Now if we died with Christ, we believe that we
will also live with him. For we know that since Christ
was raised from the dead, he cannot die again;
death no longer has mastery over him.

—Romans 6:8–9

Were You There?

Traditional   Traditional Spiritual

1. Were you there when they cru-ci-fied my Lord? Were you
2. Were you there when they nailed Him to a tree? Were you
3. Were you there when they laid Him in a tomb? Were you
4. Were you there when He rose up from the dead? Were you

there when they cru-ci-fied my Lord? O_____
there when they nailed Him to a tree? O_____
there when they laid Him in a tomb? O_____
there when He rose up from the dead? O_____

some-times it caus-es me to trem-ble, trem-ble, trem-ble!
some-times it caus-es me to trem-ble, trem-ble, trem-ble!
some-times it caus-es me to trem-ble, trem-ble, trem-ble!
some-times I feel like shout-ing glo-ry, glo-ry, glo-ry!

Were you there when they cru-ci-fied my Lord?
Were you there when they nailed Him to a tree?
Were you there when they laid Him in a tomb?
Were you there when He rose up from the dead?

*F*olk songs are generally described as expressing the heartfelt traditions and experiences of a particular culture or people. They become, therefore, greatly cherished by each succeeding generation.

"Were You There?" is one of our most popular spirituals. It was probably the first spiritual of African-American origin to appear in American hymnals. Like most folk pieces, it has no single author and no single composer. It simply evolved out of community life and worship, first appearing in 1907 in Frederick J. Work's *Folk Songs of the American Negroes.*

Spirituals represent some of the finest in American folk music and are one of America's most significant contributions to sacred song expressions. Profound in their simplicity, these songs are usually a blending of African heritage, remembrances of harsh slavery experiences, and a very personal interpretation of biblical stories and truths. They reflect so well the religious attitudes and aspirations of much of black America.

Spirituals, often sung without any instrumental accompaniment, carry the feeling of being present and very much involved in the incident portrayed. Christ's suffering, death, and resurrection become an intense experience, expressed in song with much emotion and freedom of spirit.

Through this spiritual, we realize that the redemptive work of Christ requires more than our mental assent. We see ourselves as active participants in the entire story of redemption. The biblical account of the cross becomes a personal conviction, and our very souls are gripped by its emotional power.

Sometimes it causes me to tremble . . .
Sometimes I feel like shouting glory, glory, glory . . .

---

*Imagine that you were standing at the foot of the cross
when Christ was tortured and crucified. Then place
yourself outside the empty tomb when the angelic
announcement, "He is not here," was given. Try to
experience the emotions that would have been yours.*

*Come, ye saints, look here and wonder,
See the place where Jesus lay;
He has burst His bands assunder,
He has borne our sins away.*
                                        —*Thomas Kelly*

25

When I Survey the Wondrous Cross

He himself bore our sins in his body on the tree,
so that we might die to sins and live for righteousness;
by his wounds you have been healed.

—1 Peter 2:24

When I Survey the Wondrous Cross

ISAAC WATTS, 1674–1748

From a Gregorian Chant
Arr. LOWELL MASON, 1792–1872

"Hamburg"

1. When I sur - vey the won - drous cross On which the Prince of Glo - ry died, My rich - est gain I count but loss, And pour con - tempt on all my pride.
2. For - bid it, Lord, that I should boast, Save in the death of Christ, my God. All the vain things that charm me most, I sac - ri - fice them to His blood.
3. See, from His head, His hands, His feet, Sor - row and love flow min - gled down. Did e'er such love and sor - row meet, Or thorns com - pose so rich a crown?
4. Were the whole realm of na - ture mine, That were a pres - ent far too small. Love so a - maz - ing, so di - vine, De - mands my soul, my life, my all!

I glory in infirmity,
That Christ's own power may rest on me.
When I am weak, then am I strong;
Grace is my shield and Christ my song.

—Isaac Watts

his hymn by Isaac Watts—labeled by the well-known theologian Matthew Arnold as the greatest hymn in the English language—was written in 1707 for use at a Communion service conducted by Watts. It first appeared in print that same year in Watts's outstanding collection, *Hymns and Spiritual Songs*. Its original title was "Crucifixion to the World by the Cross of Christ."

In Watts's day, texts based only on personal feelings were called *hymns of human composure* and were very controversial. Almost all congregational singing at that time consisted of ponderous repetitions of the Psalms. The thoughts presented by Watts in these lines must have pointed eighteenth-century Christians to view the dying Savior in a vivid and memorable way. Surely it led them to a deeper worship experience, even as it does for us today.

Young Watts showed unusual talent at an early age, learning Latin when he was five, Greek by age nine, French by age eleven, and Hebrew by age twelve. As he grew up, he became increasingly disturbed by the uninspiring psalm singing in the English churches. He commented, "The singing of God's praise is the part of worship most closely related to heaven; but its performance among us is the worst on earth."

Throughout his life, Isaac Watts wrote more than six hundred hymns and is known today as the "father of English hymnody." All his hymns are strong and triumphant statements of the Christian faith. Yet none expresses so clear an image and genuine devotion as does this stirring and magnificent hymn text.

The melody for this text is known as the "Hamburg" tune. It was the work of Lowell Mason, who was often called the "father of American public school and church music." Mason adapted the tune in 1824 from an ancient Gregorian chant, the earliest church music known. It is of interest that the entire melody encompasses only a five-note range.

Isaac Watts's intent in writing this text was to cause Christians to think seriously about the importance of Christ's cross and the effect it should have on our lives—it "demands my soul, my life, my all."

He borrowed a room on His way to the tomb,
the Passover Lamb to eat;
They borrowed a cave for Him a grave;
they borrowed a winding sheet.
But the crown that He wore
and the cross that He bore
were His own—
The cross was His own.

— Author Unknown

From Palm Sunday to Easter

A Devotional Guide for Holy Week

Into the heart of Jesus deeper and deeper I go,
Seeking to know the reason why He should love me so—
    Why He should stoop to lift me
    Up from the miry clay,
Saving my soul, making me whole,
    Tho' I had wandered away.

—Oswald J. Smith

Who can probe fully the mystery of redemption: Jesus Christ, the Creator of the universe, suffering and dying on a Roman cross that we sinful mortals might live and reign with Him forever. We simply stand amazed and humbly respond:

O the love that sought me! O the blood that bought me!
Wondrous grace that brought me to the fold!

—W. Spencer Walton

It is spiritually profitable for believers to review often the events of Holy Week—Christ's suffering, death, and bodily resurrection as recorded in all four Gospels. We should allow our minds to be saturated with these compelling truths until our souls vibrate with gratitude and joyous anticipation:

And thru' eternal ages gratefully I shall sing,
"O how He loved! O how He loved!
Jesus, my Lord and my King!"
—Oswald. J. Smith.

The following pages give a day-by-day walk through the events of Holy Week with suggested Scripture readings, songs, and devotional thoughts. They are included here as a means of enriching your celebration of Christ's redemption—during the Easter season especially, but also at any other time of the year.

May this devotional journey through the events of Easter week quicken our devotion to Christ and move each of us to truly worship and praise Him for the redemption that is ours to enjoy, both now and eternally. Hallelujah, what a Savior!

Palm Sunday—*A Day of Triumph and Tears*

Observations and Highlights

1. Crowds of people had recently converged on Jerusalem for the privilege of celebrating the Passover in this hallowed city.
2. Matthew (21:4) reminds us that the events of this day were in fulfillment of Old Testament prophecy.

> *Rejoice greatly, O Daughter of Zion! Shout, Daughter of Jerusalem! See, your king comes to you, righteous and having salvation, gentle and riding on a donkey, on a colt, the foal of a donkey.*
> –Zechariah 9:9

3. As Jesus approached Jerusalem on the donkey, He wept over the sinful condition of the people. He also knew that in a few years, A.D. 70, the city would be destroyed by the Romans (Matt. 23:37–39).
4. Jesus was giving the Jewish nation one final opportunity to accept Him as their king and promised Messiah. Yet, as God, He knew

that those who were chanting their "Hosannas" would in a few brief days be part of a frantic mob shouting "Crucify Him!"

> Ride on! ride on in majesty! Hark! all the tribes hosanna cry;
> Thy humble beast pursues his road
>   with palms and scattered garments strowed.
> Ride on! ride on in majesty! In lowly pomp ride on to die;
> O Christ, Thy triumphs now begin
>   o'er captive death and conquered sin.
> Ride on! Ride on in Majesty!
> —Henry Hart Milman

5. At the end of this Sunday—a day of temporary triumph mixed with compassionate tears—Jesus and His disciples returned to Bethany, a little village about two miles east of Jerusalem.

Suggested Bible Readings

Matthew 21:1–11; 23:37–38; Mark 11:1–11; Luke 19:29–44; John 12:12–19

Suggested Hymns

Hosanna, Loud Hosanna—page 45
All Glory, Laud, and Honor—page 11

Monday—*A Day of Authority*

Observations and Highlights

1. Early in the morning while returning with His disciples to Jerusalem, Jesus saw a fig tree. It should have been capable of satisfying their hunger, but a closer examination of the tree revealed branches thick with foliage but bearing no fruit. Disappointed, Jesus placed a curse on the tree:

> *May no one ever eat fruit from you again.*
> —Mark 11:14

Immediately the tree withered.

—Matthew 21:19

2. Jesus entered the temple and encountered men selling cattle, sheep, and doves while other men were exchanging money. He spoke these words of rebuke:

How dare you turn my Father's house into a market!

—John 2:16

"My house will be called a house of prayer," but you are making it "a den of robbers."

—Matthew 21:13

3. Jesus proceeded to drive all the commercial dealers out of the temple with a whip of cords and pronounced this judgment:

Your house is left to you desolate.

—Matthew 23:38

4. A fig tree (or a person) that does not fulfill its (his or her) intended purpose of bearing fruit still incurs the displeasure of our Lord. The same is true of a house of worship that has lost its virtue.
5. Jesus and His disciples return to Bethany.

Suggested Bible Readings

Isaiah 56:7; Jeremiah 7:11; Matthew 21:18–22; Mark 11:12–19; John 2:13–25; 15:16

Suggested Hymns

Lead Me to Calvary—page 67
When I Survey the Wondrous Cross—page 107

Tuesday—*A Day of Controversy*

Observations and Highlights

1. This was perhaps one of the busiest and most intense days of Jesus' earthly ministry.
2. While Jesus was teaching the people in the temple court, the Jewish leaders confronted Him with a challenge.

> *By what authority are you doing these things? . . . Who gave you this authority?*
>
> —Matthew 21:23

3. Jesus delivered seven scathing "woes" against the religious leaders, using such harsh terms as "hypocrites," "blind guides," "snakes," and "brood of vipers."
4. Jesus taught His disciples a lesson in giving, using the example of a poor widow woman who had just given "two very small copper coins . . . out of her poverty" (Mark 12:42, 44).
5. Jesus taught Peter, James, John, and Andrew what some of the signs would be for the end times. He then gave them (and us) this warning:

> *Be careful, or your hearts will be weighed down with dissipation, drunkenness and the anxieties of life, and that day will close on you unexpectedly like a trap.*
>
> —Luke 21:34

6. The religious rulers' conspiracy with Judas was about to develop.
7. Jesus and the disciples returned to Bethany after a long and difficult day.

Suggested Bible Readings

Matthew 21:18–27; 24:3–25, 46; 26:1–4; Mark 11:27–33; 12:41–44; 13; 14:1–2, 10–11; Luke 20:1–8, 45–47; 21:1–38; 22:1–6

Suggested Hymns

There Is a Green Hill Far Away—page 95
Majestic Sweetness Sits Enthroned—page 75

Wednesday—*A Day for Retreat*

Observations and Highlights

1. Very little is known of what Jesus did or said on this day. No doubt Jesus and the disciples remained and rested in Bethany from Tuesday evening until Thursday afternoon. Knowing what lay ahead, Jesus likely desired this time of rest before facing the coming days. He might also have used this day to instruct His disciples about the task of carrying on their ministries after His departure.

2. "While he was in Bethany, reclining at the table in the home of a man known as Simon the Leper, a woman came with an alabaster jar of very expensive perfume, made of pure nard. She broke the jar and poured the perfume on his head" (Mark 14:3).

3. Jesus rebuked those who complained that the woman's gesture was an exorbitant waste and that the money should have been used to help the poor.

4. Jesus reminded them and us that deeds of love for Him will not be forgotten.

> *I tell you the truth, wherever the gospel is preached throughout the world, what she has done will also be told, in memory of her.*
> —Mark 14:9

5. What a contrast is given here between the woman's outpouring of sincere love for Christ and the conniving of Judas as he planned the betrayal for personal gain. A note of interest: the perfume is estimated to have been worth twice as much as the thirty pieces of silver Judas received.

Suggested Bible Readings
Psalm 22; Isaiah 53; Mark 14:1–10

Suggested Hymns
My Jesus, I Love Thee—page 79
Blessed Redeemer—page 19
Jesus Paid It All—page 63

Thursday—*A Day of Remembrance*

Observations and Highlights

1. This day has become known among Christians as Maundy Thursday, from the Latin *mandatum*, meaning mandate or command. Jesus gave His disciples the mandate to love one another even as He had demonstrated His love for them. A loving relationship among the followers of Christ is a mark of true discipleship.

2. It was the Lord's desire to celebrate the Jewish Passover with His disciples and to initiate the new covenant, symbolized by the elements of the Communion service or Lord's Supper.

> *Whenever you eat this bread or drink of this cup, you are proclaiming that the Lord has died for you, and you will do that until he comes again.*
> —1 Corinthians 11:26 (PHILLIPS)

3. The Passover meal, consisting of unleavened bread, bitter herbs, wine, and the paschal lamb, was the Jewish celebration of the night in Egypt when the death angel passed over the Israelites and they were delivered by Jehovah from four hundred years of Egyptian bondage.

4. At the supper, the disciples began disputing among themselves about their individual importance. Jesus then taught them the lesson of servanthood by washing their feet (Luke 22:24; John 13:4).

5. Judas was revealed as the traitor (John 13:26).

But the hand of him who is going to betray me is with mine on the table.

—Luke 22:21

6. The Lord gave His farewell message to His disciples: Matthew 26:31–35; Mark 14:27–31; Luke 22:31–38; John 13:31; 16:33
7. Peter's denial of Jesus was foretold:

Before the rooster crows, you will disown me three times!

—John 13:38

8. The Lord said an intercessory prayer for Himself, for His disciples, and for all believers (John 17).
9. Jesus joined the disciples in singing a closing psalm of praise. This was likely one of the Hallel Psalms (113–118).
10. Jesus, with His disciples, left for the garden to pray.

Father, if you are willing, take this cup from me; yet not my will, but yours be done.

—Luke 22:42

Suggested Bible Readings

Psalms 115–118; Matthew 26:17–35; Mark 14:12–31; Luke 22:7–34; John 13:1–17; 17; 1 Corinthians 11:23–26

Suggested Hymns

'Tis Midnight; and on Olive's Brow—page 99
In the Hour of Trial—page 59
Let Us Break Bread Together—page 71

Friday—*A Day of Suffering*

Observations and Highlights

1. The day is called Good Friday, not because of what happened on

that day but because of the good that Christ accomplished for the lost human race.

2. Very likely, many of the events prior to Christ's crucifixion occurred between late Thursday evening and daybreak Friday: the agony of Gethsemane, the betrayal and arrest of Jesus, the trials before the Jewish authorities and later before Herod and Pilate, Peter's denial in the courtyard of the high priest, the suicide of Judas.

3. For the crucifixion, Jesus was taken outside the city walls to a place called Golgotha—a place of the skull. Here the cruelest Roman instrument of death became God's method of reconciling humankind with Himself.

4. The seven utterances of Christ from the cross were:

   a. "Father, forgive them" (Luke 23:34).
   b. "Today you will be with me in paradise" (Luke 23:43).
   c. "Dear woman, here is your son. . . . Here is your mother" (John 19:26–27).
   d. "My God, my God, why have you forsaken me?" (Matt. 27:46).
   e. "I am thirsty" (John 19:28).
   f. "It is finished" (John 19:30).
   g. "Father, into your hands I commit my spirit" (Luke 23:46).

5. Four miraculous events occurred during the crucifixion of Jesus.

   a. Darkness covered the land for three hours.
   b. The veil of the temple was rent in two from the bottom to the top.
   c. The earth shook and the rocks were split.
   d. The graves were opened and the bodies of many holy people were raised to life.

   When the centurion and those with him who were guarding Jesus saw the earthquake and all that had happened, they were terrified, and exclaimed, "Surely he was the Son of God!"
   —Matthew 27:54

6. For His burial, Jesus' body was placed in a new tomb owned by

Joseph of Arimathea, a secret follower of Jesus. Joseph was assisted by Nicodemus, also a secret believer, who helped prepare the body for burial.

Suggested Bible Readings
Isaiah 53; Matthew 26 and 27; Mark 14 and 15; Luke 23; John 18 and 19

Suggested Hymns
There Is a Fountain—page 91
O Sacred Head, Now Wounded—page 83
Were You There?—page 103

Saturday—*A Day of Silence*

Observations and Highlights

1. This was the Jewish Sabbath, a day of rest—a calm before the stir of resurrected life.
2. It was a day of melancholy for the disciples and followers of Jesus. Their hopes for a new Jewish kingdom lay buried in a tomb.
3. It was a day of concern for the Jewish and Roman authorities.

> *His disciples may come and steal the body and tell the people that he has been raised from the dead. This last deception will be worse than the first.*
>
> —Matthew 27:64

4. Where was the spirit of Jesus while His body was in the grave? Some students of Scripture submit that from the time of His death to the moment of His resurrection, Jesus and the repentant thief visited the unseen abode of departed human spirits. This abode had two compartments: "hades" or "sheol," the place of the unrighteous; and "paradise" or "Abraham's bosom," the place of the righteous. Since the ascension of Christ, the departed non-repentant souls have gone directly to hell to await their final judgment and

the eternal "lake of fire" (Rev. 20:14). The redeemed in Christ, however, have gone directly to heaven and into the immediate presence of God (2 Cor. 12:1–4).

Upon His death, then, it is thought that Jesus descended into hades to set the doom of the nonrepentant (1 Peter 3:19). He also visited paradise with the repentant thief from the cross (Luke 23:43). With His ascension forty days later, Jesus "led captivity captive" (Eph. 4:8 KJV), and all who have since died trusting in His redemptive work now go directly to heaven.

We affirm this teaching, at least in part, when we state the Apostles' Creed (the traditional summary of Christian belief) in our services of worship.

> . . . *suffered under Pontius Pilate, was crucified, dead, and buried; He descended into hell. . . .*

Suggested Bible Readings

Habakkuk 2:5; Matthew 11:23; 27:62–65; Luke 16:19–31; 23:55; John 14:1–14

Suggested Hymns

Beneath the Cross of Jesus—page 15
In the Cross of Christ I Glory—page 55
The Strife Is O'er—page 87

Easter Sunday—*The Day of Final Victory!*

"Alleluia" the choir is chanting with joyous, jubilant voice.
"The Lord is risen! is risen! Rejoice, rejoice, rejoice!"
From the tomb in which men laid Him the stone is rolled away,
And lo! the Christ they sing of is here in our midst today.
                                                    —Eben E. Rexford

Observations and Highlights

1. Easter—the day when all the Old Testament prophecies and all of the preceding New Testament events in the unfolding of redemption's story came together in one climactic announcement:

    He is not here; he has risen, just as he said.
    —Matthew 28:6

2. Every Sunday—the Lord's Day—is a celebration and proclamation of Christ's victory over death.
3. The resurrection of Christ is a historic and documented fact. Our Lord confirmed it with various personal appearances on resurrection Sunday.

    a. To the other women (Matthew 28:8–10)
    b. To Mary Magdalene (Mark 16:9–11)
    c. To two of His followers on their return to Emmaus, one whose name was Cleopas (Luke 24:13–33)
    d. To Simon Peter (Luke 24:34)
    e. To the ten disciples (Luke 24:36–43)

4. Within the next forty days, Christ made numerous other appearances, including one to the five hundred "at the same time" (1 Cor. 15:6).
5. The open grave is God's pledge to us as believers that we too shall be victorious over death and will live eternally with Him (John 11:25).

    O death, where is thy sting? O grave, where is thy victory?
    —1 Corinthians 15:55 (KJV)

6. After resurrection Sunday, the disciples and the other followers of Christ proclaimed the Good News—"Jesus and the resurrection" (Acts 17:18)—with a new authority, power, and joy.
7. The resurrected, living Christ is still the very heartbeat of the church's ministry. There is no salvation apart from personally believing this truth:

If you confess with your mouth, "Jesus is Lord," and believe in your heart that God raised him from the dead, you will be saved.
—Romans 10:9

And if Christ has not been raised, your faith is futile; you are still in your sins.
—1 Corinthians 15:17

Suggested Bible Readings

Isaiah 53:9–12; Matthew 28:1–10; Mark 16:1–14; Luke 24:1–2, 13–32; John 20:1–19; 1 Corinthians 15:3–8, 14–17

> The Savior lives, no more to die;
> He lives our Head, enthroned on high.
> He lives triumphant o'er the grave;
> He lives eternally to save.
> He lives to still His people's fears;
> He lives to wipe away their tears.
> He lives their mansions to prepare;
> He lives to bring them safely there,
> Then let our souls in Him rejoice,
> And sing His praise with cheerful voice;
> Our doubts and fears forever gone,
> For Christ is on the Father's throne.
> —Samuel Medley

Suggested Hymns

Christ the Lord Is Risen Today—page 27
Christ Arose—page 23
He Lives—page 39
I Know That My Redeemer Liveth—page 49
Abide with Me—page 7
Crown Him with Many Crowns—page 31
Hallelujah, What a Savior!—page 35

Amazing Grace
366 Inspiring Hymn Stories for Daily Devotions
0-8254-3425-4   400 pages
Over 200,000 copies in print. Each day's devotional highlights biblical truths drawn from the true-life experiences behind the writing of these well-known hymns. Each story contains a portion of the hymn itself, as well as suggested Scripture readings, meditations, and practical applications. Here's a devotional to get excited about!

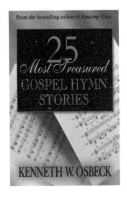

25 Most Treasured Gospel Hymn Stories
0-8254-3430-0   112 pages
Kenneth Osbeck tells the dramatic story behind 25 gospel songs and ends each section with a thoughtful reflection that lends even greater meaning to these all-time favorites.

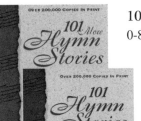

101 Hymn Stories
0-8254-3416-5   288 pages

101 More Hymn Stories
0-8254-3420-3   328 pages

Thrilling collections of the stories behind your favorite hymns. The exciting events that produced such classic expressions of praise as "A Mighty Fortress," "Fairest Lord Jesus," "How Great Thou Art," "Jesus Loves Me," "Holy, Holy, Holy," "Rock of Ages," and "The Old Rugged Cross" are brought to life in vivid, inspiring detail.

Amazing Grace (gift edition)
Illustrated Stories of Favorite Hymns
0-8254-3433-5   64 pages
This colorful illustrated edition includes 28 of the most popular hymn story devotionals from the best-selling *Amazing Grace*.